THE HANDS-ON
MARVELOUS BALL BOOK

Bradford Hansen-Smith

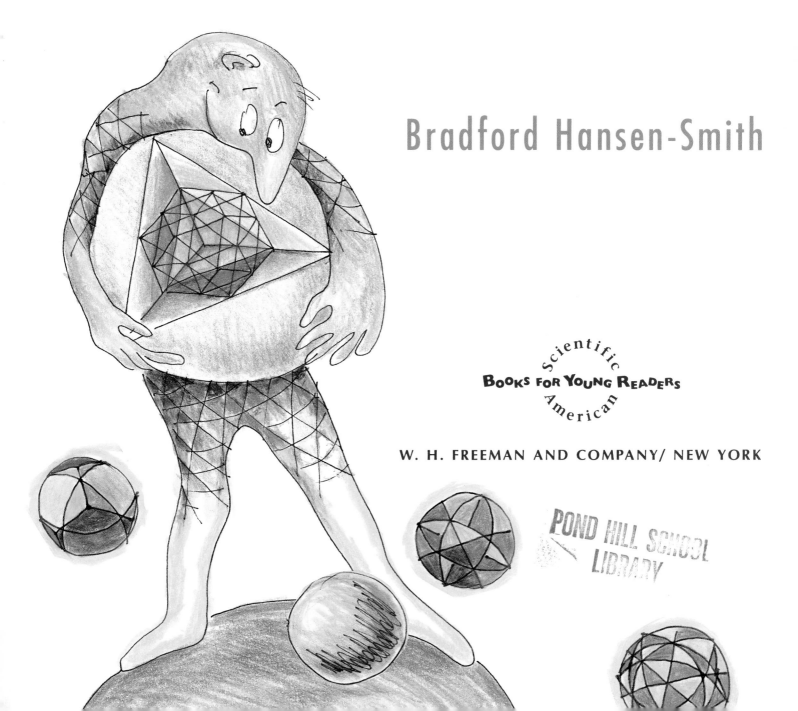

Scientific
BOOKS FOR YOUNG READERS
American

W. H. FREEMAN AND COMPANY/ NEW YORK

To all children, towards understanding
the WHOLENESS of where we all are.

—B. H-S.

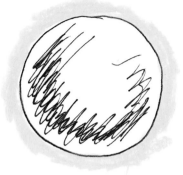

Scientific American Books for Young Readers is an imprint of
W. H. Freeman and Company, 41 Madison Avenue, New York, NY 10010.

Book design by Debora Smith

Library of Congress Cataloging-in-Publication Data

Hansen-Smith, Bradford.

The hands-on marvelous ball book / by Bradford Hansen-Smith.

ISBN 0-7167-6628-0 (hard cover)

1. Geometry—Juvenile literature. 2. Paper work—Juvenile literature.
[1. Geometry. 2. Paper work 3. Handicraft.] I. Title.

QA445.5.H36   1995   95-14413

516'.15—dc20   CIP

                                                         AC

Printed in Hong Kong

10 9 8 7 6 5 4 3 2 1

Jimmy found a ball
Rolling on the ground.
Isn't that strange
Without a hill around?

So he thought, "This cannot be.
There is no reason I can see
Why a ball is rolling 'round
With no pushing to be found."

The ball then hopped into the air.
Slowly spinning around up there,
It looked just like a planet place
Right in front of Jimmy's face.

Suddenly, stranger than before,
It looked like two,
It looked like four.

The outside still out,
The inside still in—
Yet it looked not at all
Like the ball it had been.

It was moving and wiggling—
Stretching out wide—
Losing its shape
Without losing Inside.

"Now I can go in,
But I'm still out, you see,
Because the ball is a whole
With holes in it for me."

This whole-ball-four
Grew as small as a pea,
Then soooooooO big
It was hard to see.

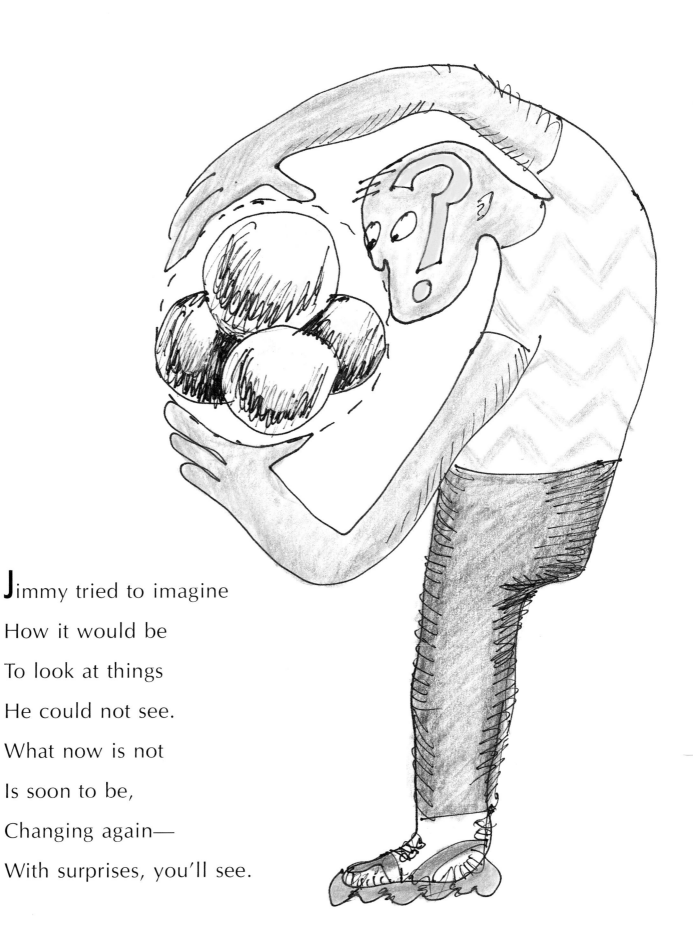

Jimmy tried to imagine

How it would be

To look at things

He could not see.

What now is not

Is soon to be,

Changing again—

With surprises, you'll see.

The ball disappeared, and in its place

Was a pattern of points, floating in space.

Four were the centers,

Six where they touched,

Ten points altogether.

Jimmy said, "That's not much."

Hovering above the ground,

The pattern slowly turned around.

The six points moved one way,

The centers another,

Making two forms—

One part of the other.

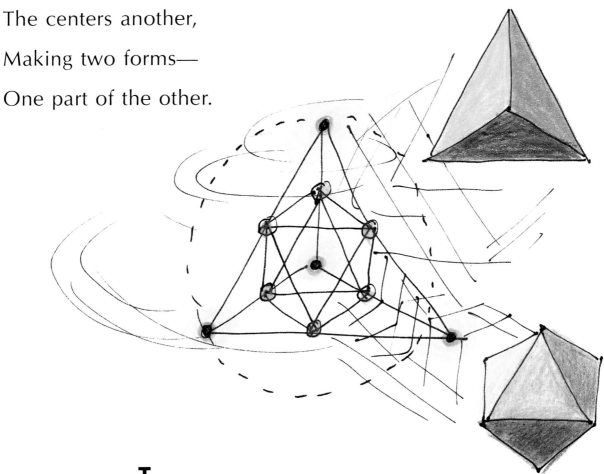

The tetrahedron, a red form,

The octahedron, a green.

The difference between the forms

In two colors could be seen.

The ball was now gone with two forms in its place,

Where each was the other in each other's space.

The two things were different,

Two aspects of one.

"This transforming ball is a whole lot of fun."

Quick as can be, they both made a change;

Their insides and outsides were rearranged.

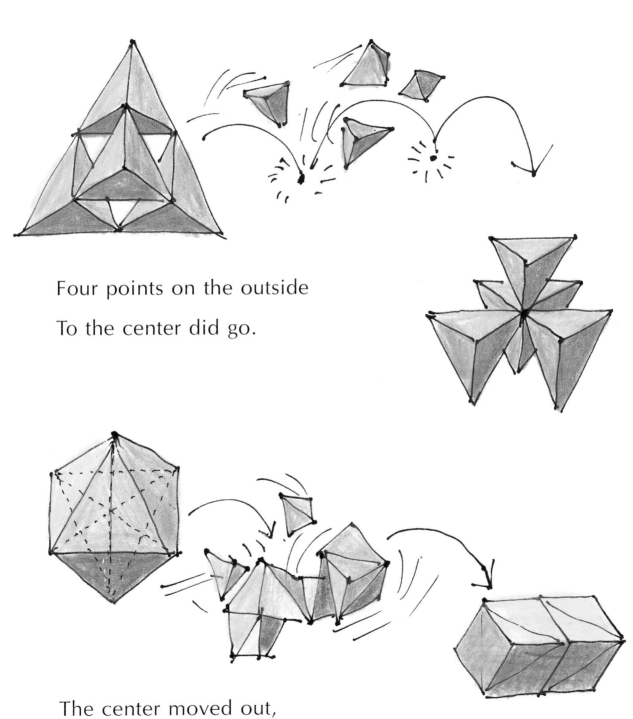

Four points on the outside

To the center did go.

The center moved out,

Making eight corners show.

After all of the changing and moving about,

Upside and downside, inside and out,

Both joined together in one solid clump

And sat on the floor,

Center and front—

A four-cornered,

Two-colored,

Triangular

Bump.

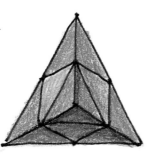

All of a sudden it started to shake,

Tremble and shiver,

Quiver and quake.

In no time at all there were hundreds around,

Shaping and shuffling to a very soft sound.

Over and under,

Into and out,

Transforming, reforming—

All and about.

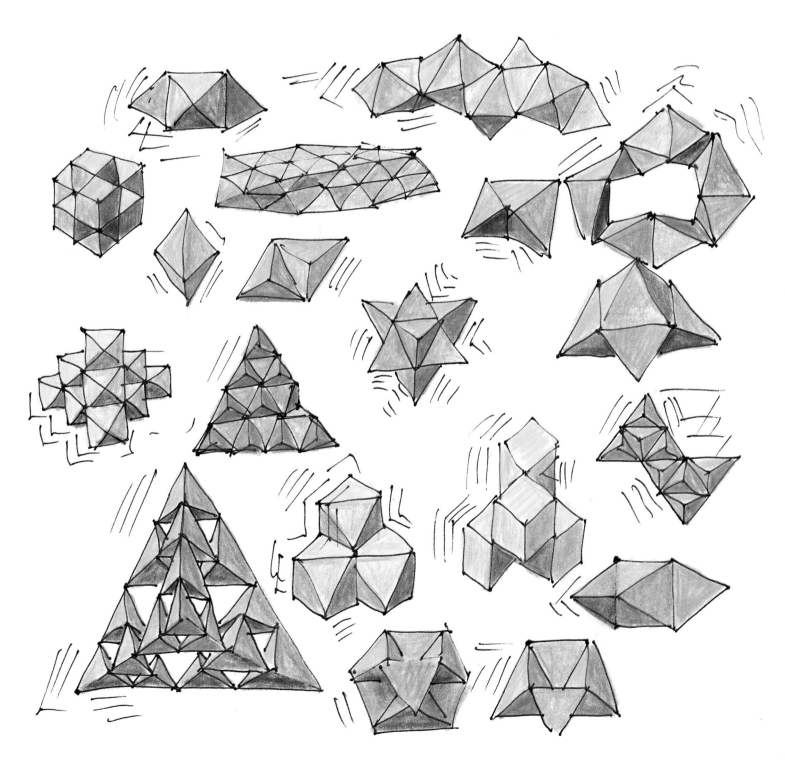

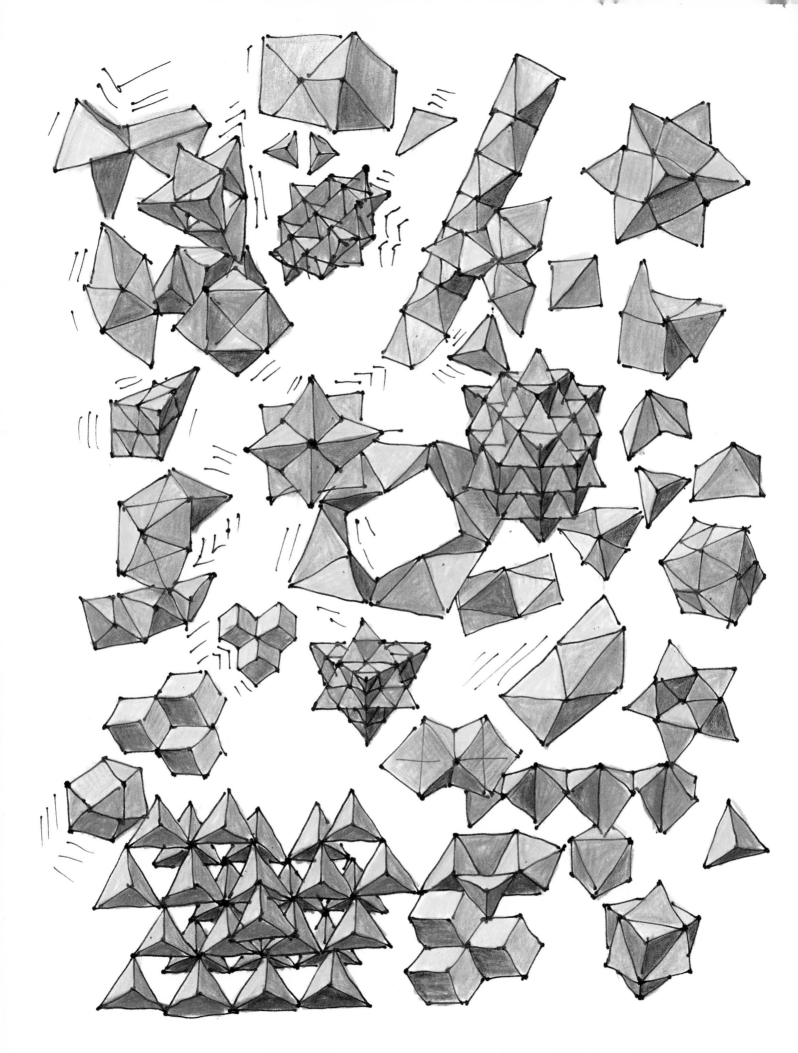

With his confusion

Beginning to clear,

Jimmy grinned from ear to ear.

"All of these things come from a sphere,

All of these wonderful things around here."

He looked at the sphere,

A circle when flat,

And said to himself,

"I can do that!

I can make all of these things from a ball.

By folding a circle

I can make them all."

And so can you—you can too.

Follow along and see what to do.

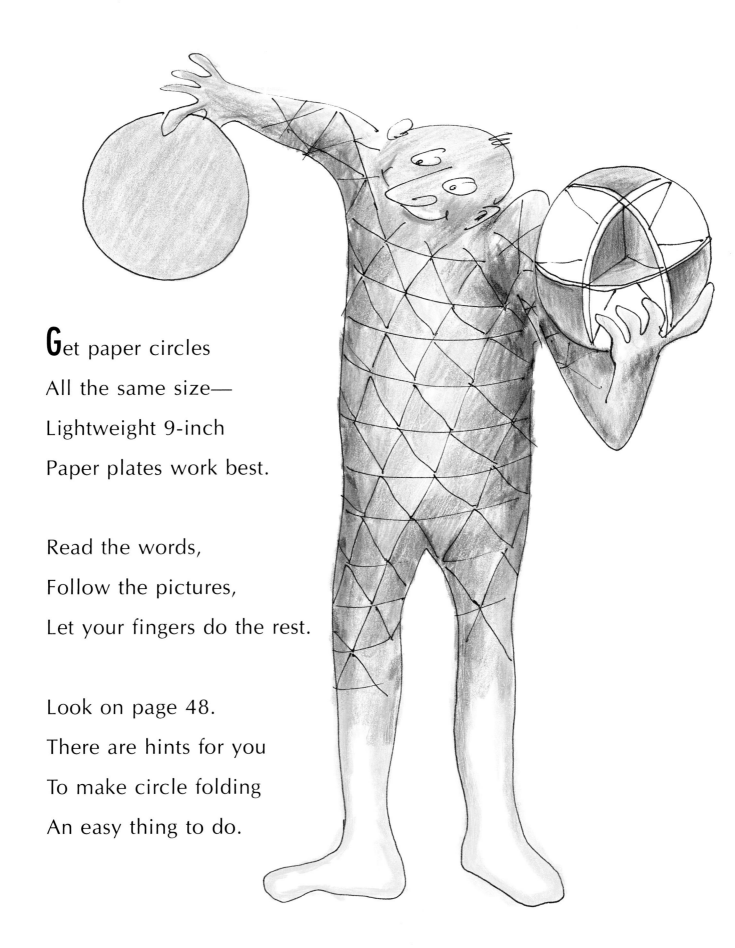

Get paper circles
All the same size—
Lightweight 9-inch
Paper plates work best.

Read the words,
Follow the pictures,
Let your fingers do the rest.

Look on page 48.
There are hints for you
To make circle folding
An easy thing to do.

THE BALL

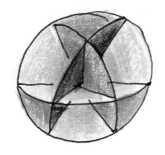

Make a ball
In a pattern called
Vector equilibrium.
Use your fingers
And your thumb,
3, 4, and 6 are all in 1.

Let's get started right away—
This is your first
Ball-making day.

Begin with a circle,
A circle is all.
Fold it in half—
Step 1 to a ball.

Fold it twice,
1 to 2,
Even up sides
And corners too.

Open the circle,
2 sets of 3,
A hexagon pattern
Is then what you'll see.
Bring together ends
Of 1 center line.
A bobby pin in the crease
Will hold it just fine.

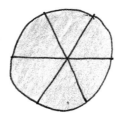
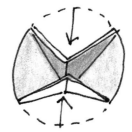

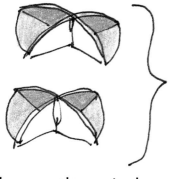
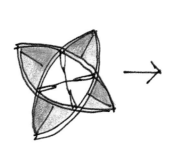

Make another circle
Exactly the same.
Put the 2 together—
Reflecting the pattern—
That is your aim.

Folding now, 2 plates more,
Put them together as before—
Joining the edges
The same as you've done,
Making 12 points—
In the center is 1.

THE TETRAHEDRON

As you did on the page before,
Fold 6 sections,
Then you'll fold more.

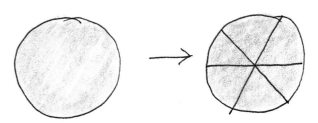

3 alternate points to the center go.
Follow the pictures;
Do what they show.

 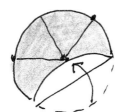 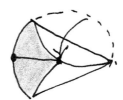 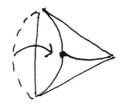 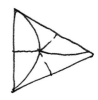

Fold each of the corner points one at a time
To the opposite edge, midpoint on the line.
Fold, then unfold, each (don't fold all at once).
Try to avoid a big messy bunch.

    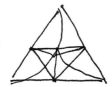

3 points fold up—
Together they come.
Tape the edges
Until you're done
Making a shape called a
Tetrahedron.

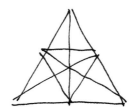 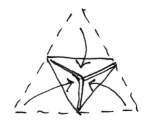

Look at the shape you now have made—
3 different ways to see—
Looking from different positions,
See 3 kinds of symmetry.

END POINT

EDGE LINE

SURFACE PLANE

There are 3 basic ways that things can touch, in multiple combinations,
3 types of joining give so many variations.

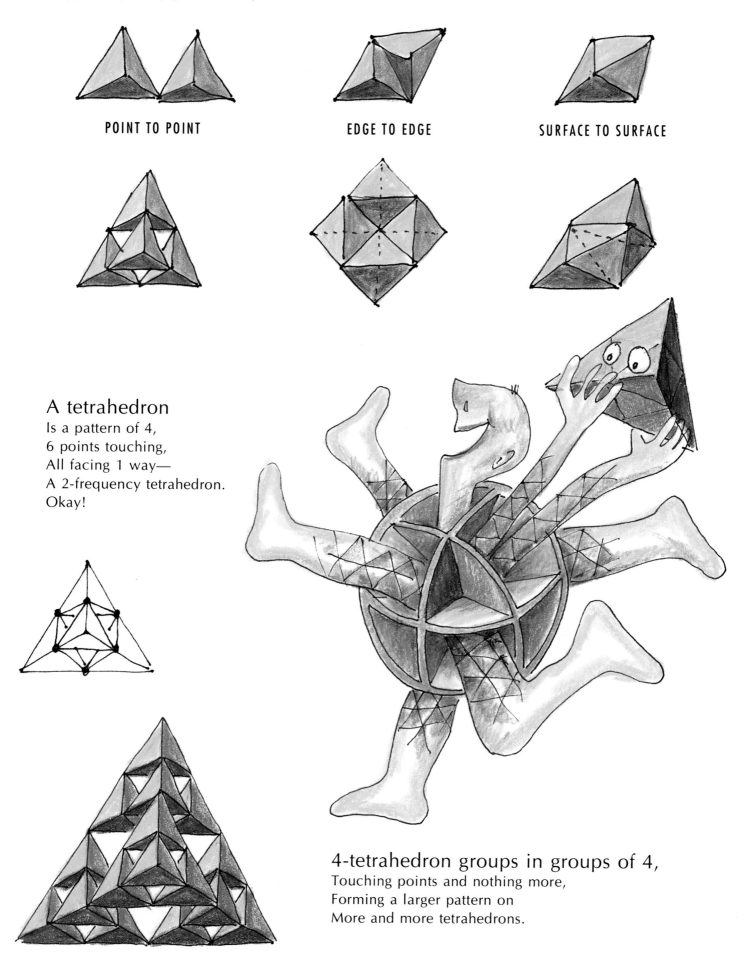

POINT TO POINT

EDGE TO EDGE

SURFACE TO SURFACE

A tetrahedron
Is a pattern of 4,
6 points touching,
All facing 1 way—
A 2-frequency tetrahedron.
Okay!

4-tetrahedron groups in groups of 4,
Touching points and nothing more,
Forming a larger pattern on
More and more tetrahedrons.

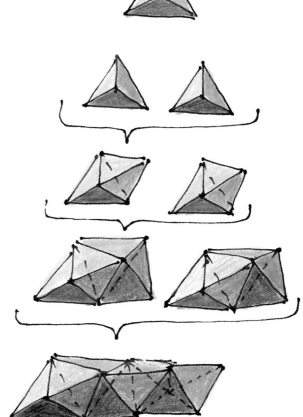

2 tetrahedrons,
Joined face to face,
Make a set of 2—
Multiplied space.

2 sets of 2
Together fit,
Making a set of 4—
That's it.

2 sets of 4
Together make
A tetrahedron
Set of 8.

8 tetrahedrons all in a line
Make a spiral of a kind,
Form it right or form it left,
Both ways work exactly best.

1, 2, 4, 8, 16, and on
Makes an endless helix
Of tetrahedrons.

Edge to edge, 2 tetrahedrons make
1 unit of 2.
Joining together 2 pair,
Make a pattern
In the form of a square.

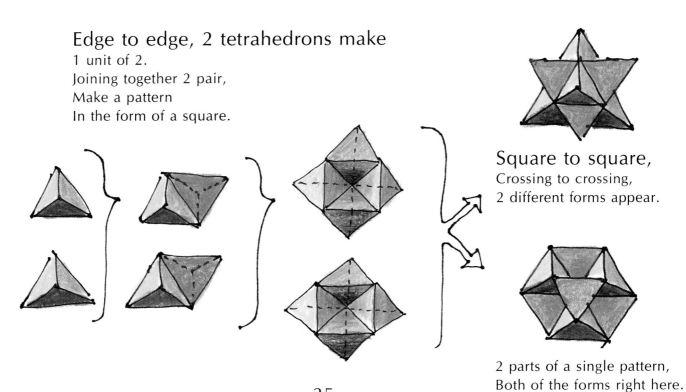

Square to square,
Crossing to crossing,
2 different forms appear.

2 parts of a single pattern,
Both of the forms right here.

THE OCTAHEDRON

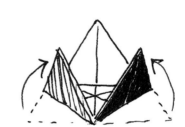

To make an octahedron,
Here is what you do—
Fold 2 plates the same
As you did in **No. 2**.

2 tetrahedrons half-open
Form triangles in and out,
Opposites together,
That's what it's about.

Taped edge to edge they fit,
Making an octahedron:
8 triangles, that's it.

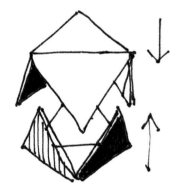
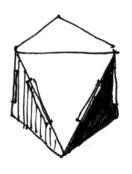
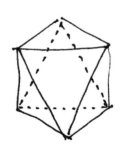

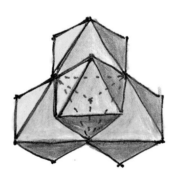
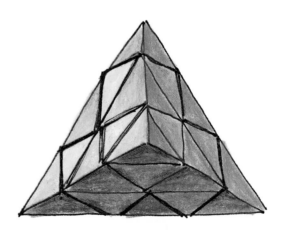

Arrange 4 octahedrons
In a tetrahedron-patterned way,
Edge to edge together.
Some tape will make them stay.
A tetrahedron space
Is the center of the 4,
With a lot of place
For tetrahedrons more.

Putting 6 tetrahedrons
In places where they fit,
With 1 more on each end,
Makes a 3-frequency tetrahedron
By adding a total of 10.

Look at the picture.
1 octahedron you'll see.
By adding 4 tetrahedrons,
Alternately,
You'll make a larger tetrahedron in place,
With an octahedron center,
It's 1-patterned space.

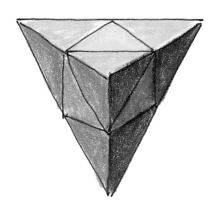

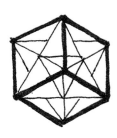

4 more tetrahedrons on the octahedron faces
Locate 8 points in just the right places
To make a cube pattern and tetrastar too.
Both of these things one thing can do.

This star form will take
9 octahedrons to tetrahedrons 8.

By adding 3 more
Octahedrons just right,
You will have 13—
Only 12 in sight.

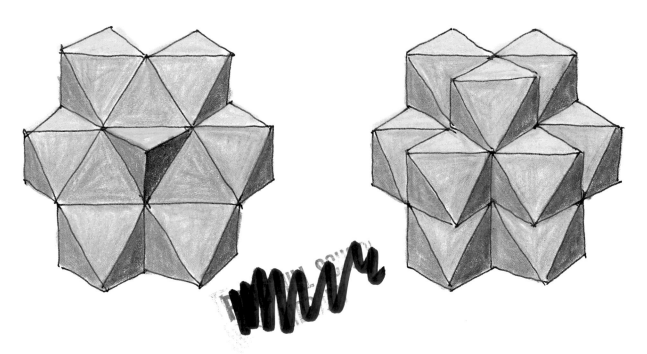

27

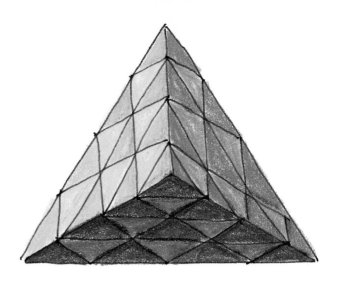

Adding tetrahedrons
Their direction all the same,

Forms another tetrahedron—
4-frequency by name.

Let's look at what's done
With 6 octahedrons in 1
That shows tetrahedronal space.

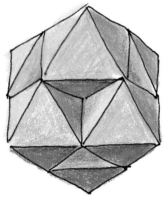

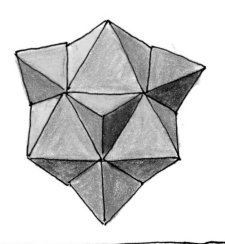

With the ends pointing in,
Filled out to the skin,
They make a solid-formed place.

Tetrahedrons turned out,
All pointing away,
Make a different thing.
Whatever it is, is what it is,
'Cause it is.
What else can you say?

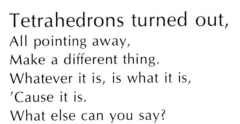

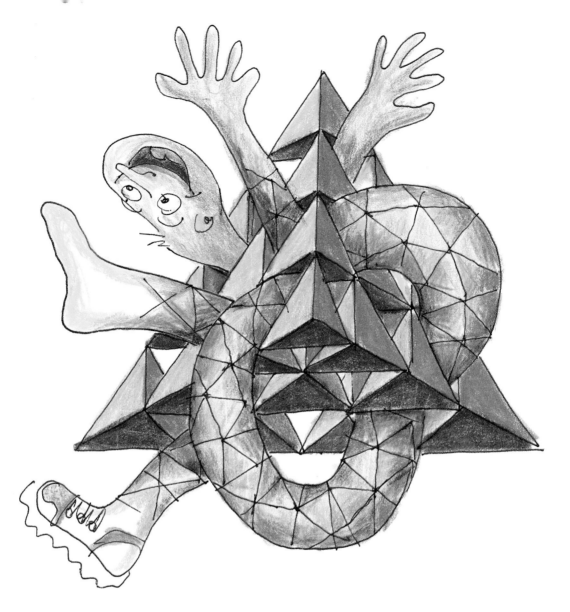

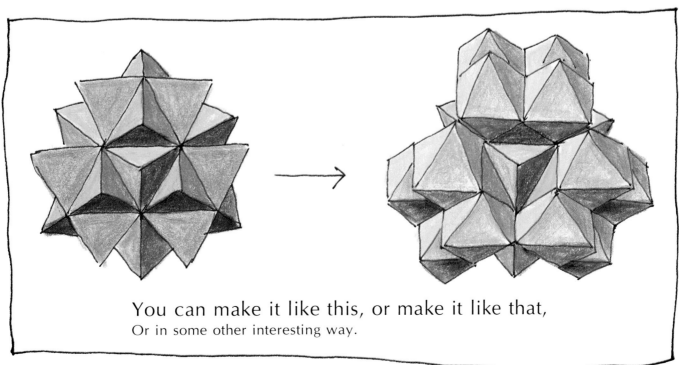

You can make it like this, or make it like that,
Or in some other interesting way.

THE RIGHT-ANGLE TETRAHEDRON

To make a right-angle tetrahedron,
Fold the tetrahedron as you did in **No. 2**.
Unfold the circle flat
And look at the pattern in front of you.

Find the large triangle,
The center 1 too,
And 6 outside points
In 3 sets of 2.

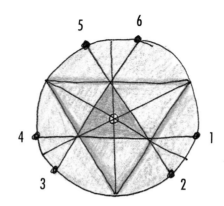

Separately fold 6 points
To the center exact.
Then open the circle,
Making it flat.

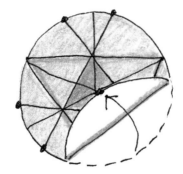

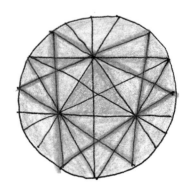

2 triangles folded on the circle line,
Crossing end points of the triangle inside,
Fold 1 of 2, either is fine.

TURN OVER

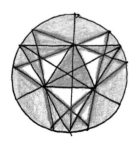  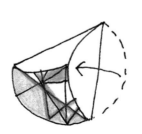 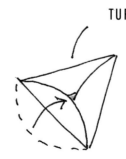 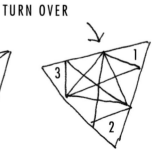

Turn over, curved edges under.
Look at the ends to see
Folded right triangles,
Counting 1, 2, 3.

Now fold the corner right triangles behind,

Using the folds of the right-angle lines.
Turn over and fold 3 ends into 1.
Tape edges closed—making a right-angle tetrahedron.

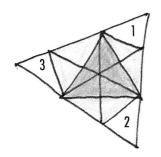 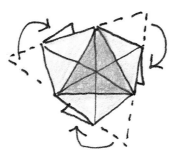 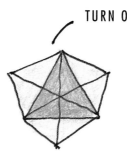

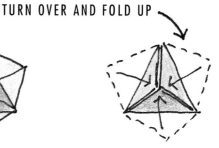

TURN OVER AND FOLD UP

Point to point,
4 right-angled tetrahedrons will go,
Making a larger one,
You know.

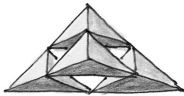

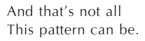

As in **No. 3**,
2 open right-angle
Tetrahedrons will be
A right-angle octahedron,
The shape you will see.

And that's not all
This pattern can be.

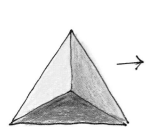 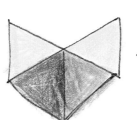 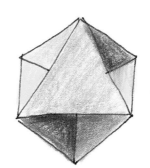 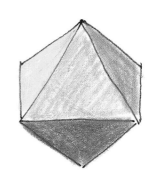

2 right-angled tetrahedrons,
Short edges joined 1 to 1.

Make another set—
An octahedron pattern
Is what you get.

Add 4 more tetrahedrons
In 4 open spaces,
Making 8 solid,
Triangular faces.

 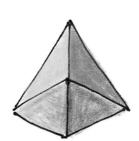 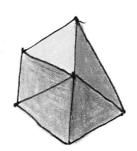 

1 tetrahedron, 1, 2, 3, 4 right-angle tetrahedrons more,
Make 1 cube
With a tetrahedron core.

Let's make a thing that's something else;
It's not one shape or the other.
It's a different thing at different times
When you twist it and fold it together.

5 tetrahedrons,
4 right-angled and a regular one,
Laid out in a row
As pictured below,
With edges taped in a hingelike way,
So it can move
And you can play.

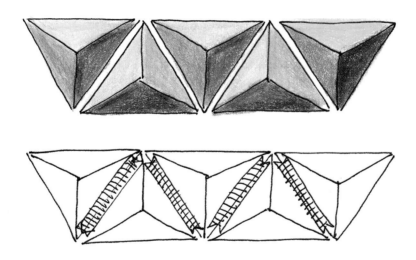

Page 48 will set you straight
On making hinges that work just great.

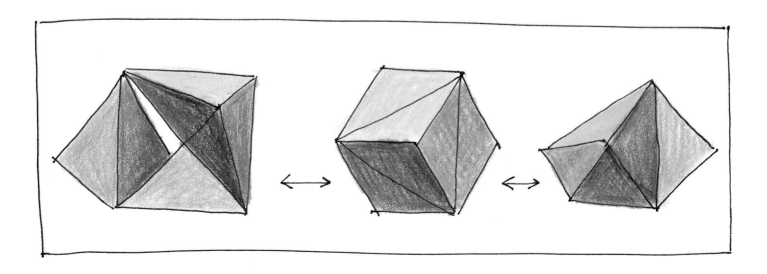

32

Make 2 of these systems exactly the same.
They are 2 parts in the whole
Circle/ball game.

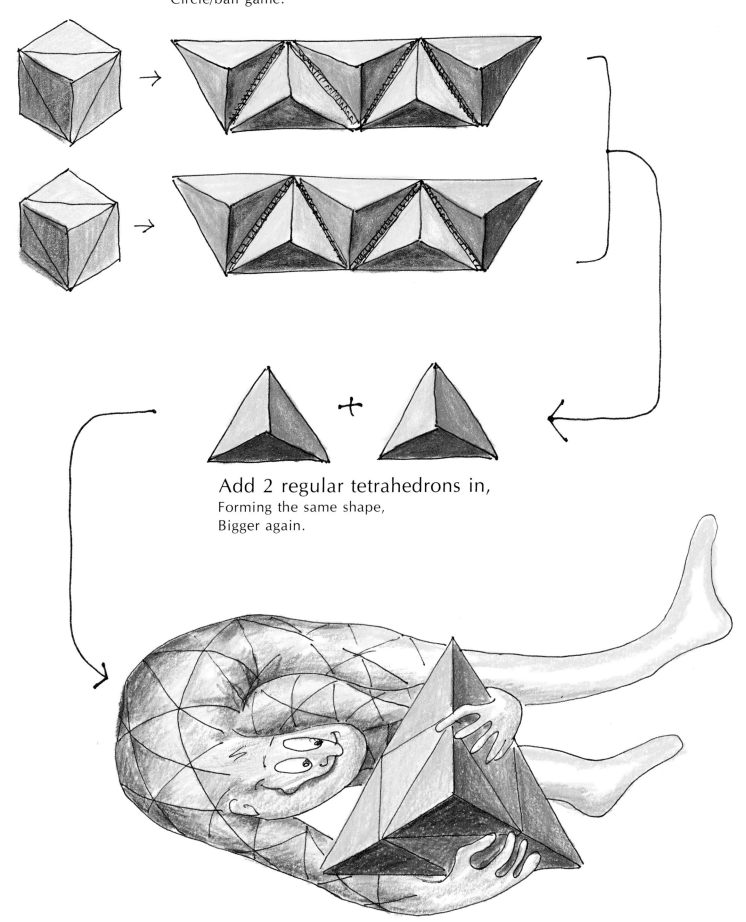

Add 2 regular tetrahedrons in,
Forming the same shape,
Bigger again.

Do what you did

On the page before.
Where there was 1
Now use 4—
Making holes,
Locating spaces,
Changing and moving
In and out places.

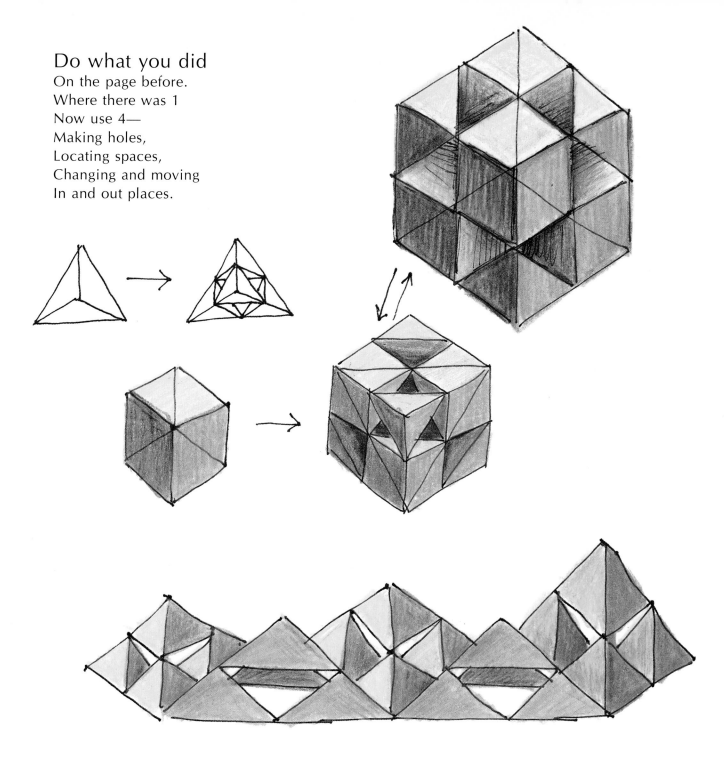

The holes and tetrahedrons

Move all around,
Flipping and flopping—
Inside, upside,
Overside, down.

Doing the things

It did before
Only doing them differently,
Doing them more,
2 to 4 to 8 then 16,
It keeps on forming
Space in between.

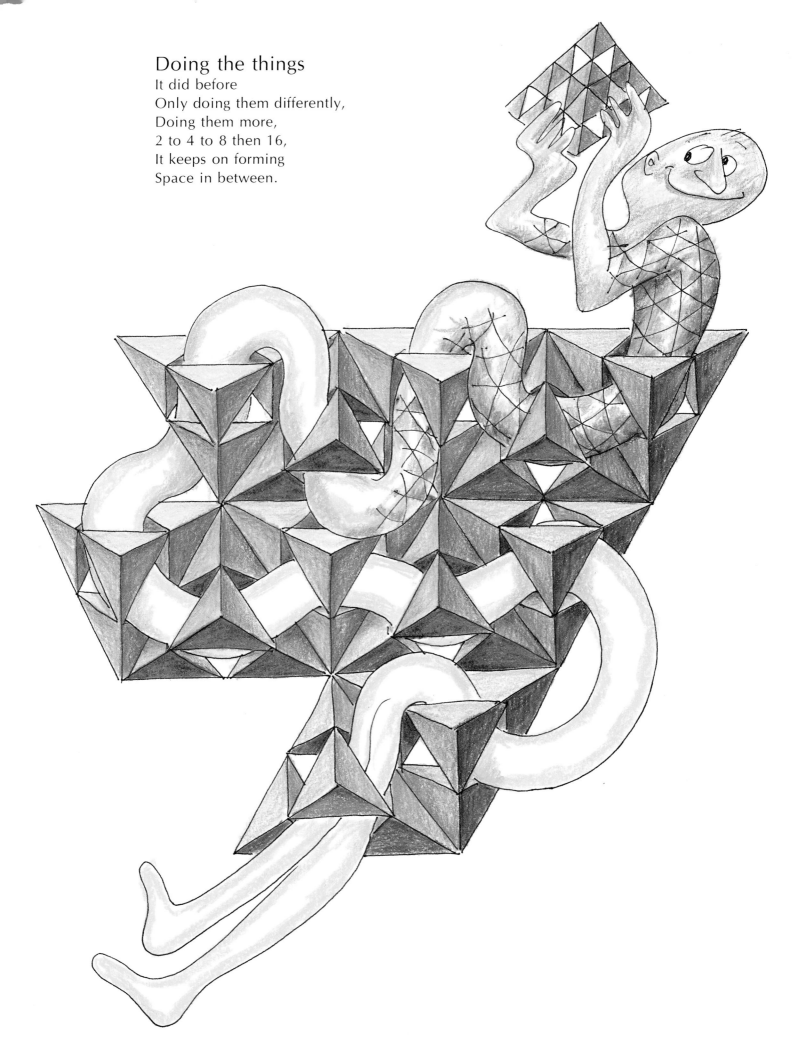

THE TORUS RING

"Now let's make a ring," Jimmy said.
"It will be fun to do."
So you can make a torus ring
And play the helix, too.

1 tetrahedron.

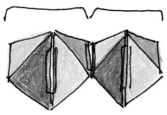

1 unit, 2 tetrahedrons make.

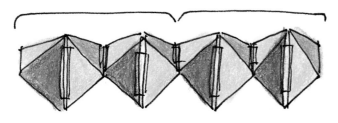

Attach 2 units of 2.

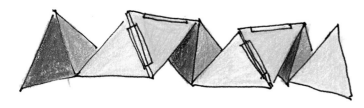

Do it again, that's what it takes,
To form a helix that moves for you.

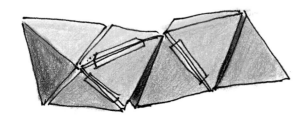

Edges to opposite edges,
8 tetrahedrons taped in a row.
Moving by hinges at 90 degrees
Is what makes this helix move so.

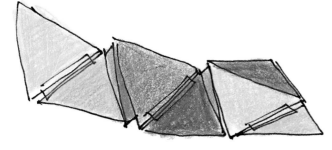

Twisting the forms,
Surface to surface,
Twisting the outside in,
Putting one half to the other,
Will alter the helical spin.

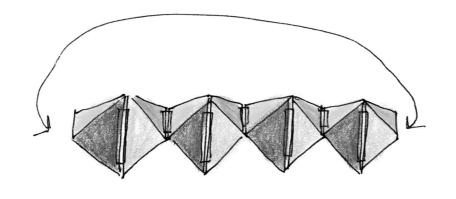

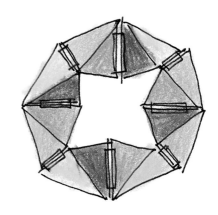

Both ends hinged together
Circle into a torus.
Outside, inside, moving through
A circling hole of movement for us.

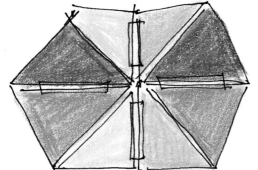

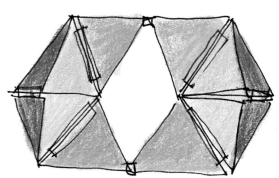

THE BALL PATTERN

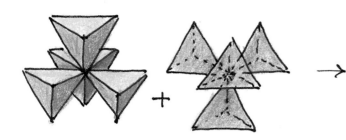

4 tetrahedrons at center touching
Make 6 spaces all the same.
2 sets in opposite directions—
Vector equilibrium by name.

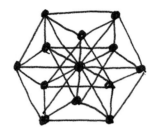

Cube octahedron is just the same,
13 points in a centered frame—
12 balls on the outside,
1 in the center location,
13 balls in order—
Now that's a celebration.

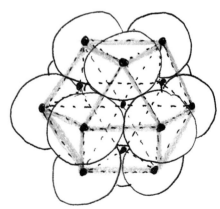

Octahedron—
1 in each square,

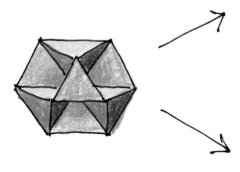

8 right-angle tetrahedrons
For each triangle there.

2 separate forms
Come together in one,
So it is called
A cube octahedron.

With this you can see
The whole ball is one.
By forming the parts,
You have only begun
Forming patterns—
Endless parts more—
All part of the parts
That happened before.

"Now I feel better,

Rounder, more whole,

And just like a ball,

I am starting to roll."

"Expanding and growing out into space,

Getting to see from my own unique place

The moving and knowing

As part of it all—

Just a small part

Of a GREAT BIG BALL."

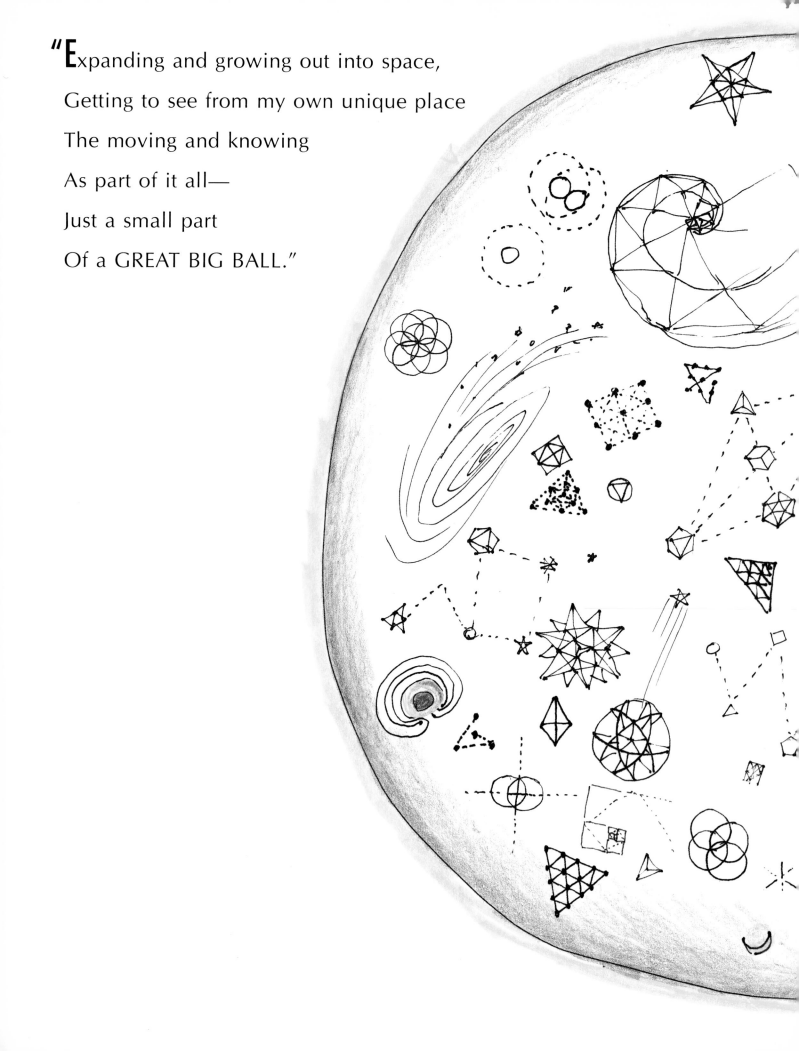

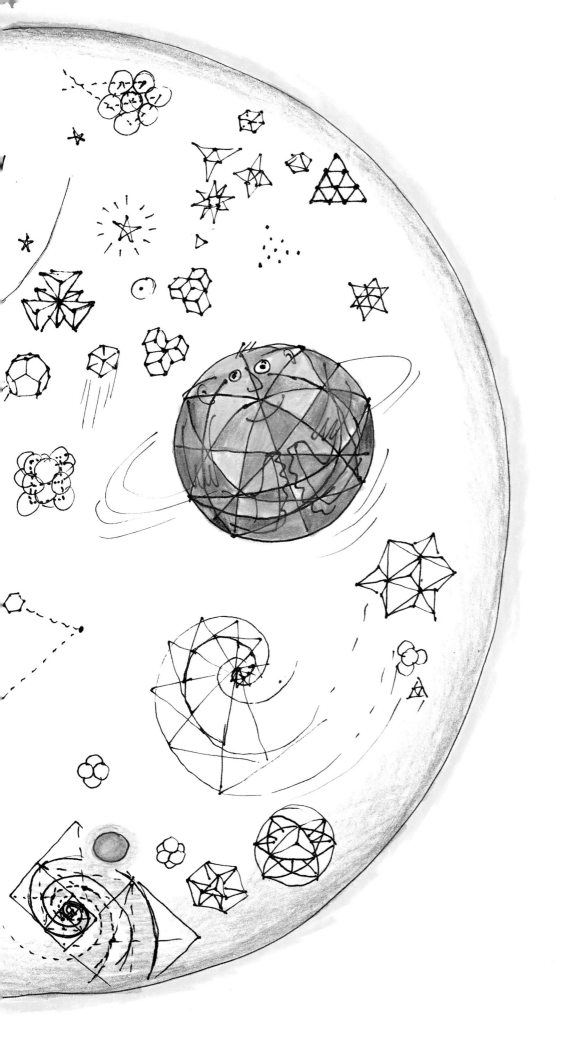

Pushing and pulling, stretch your imagination.

Think of nature as a ball-patterned configuration.

From the smallest atom to the largest star,

Nature is what/where all of us are.

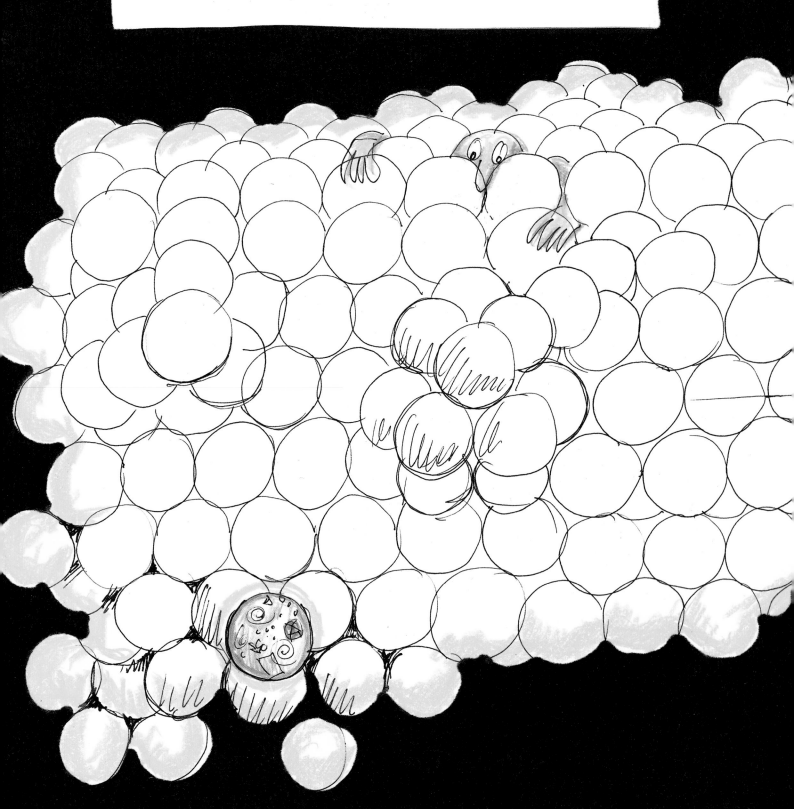

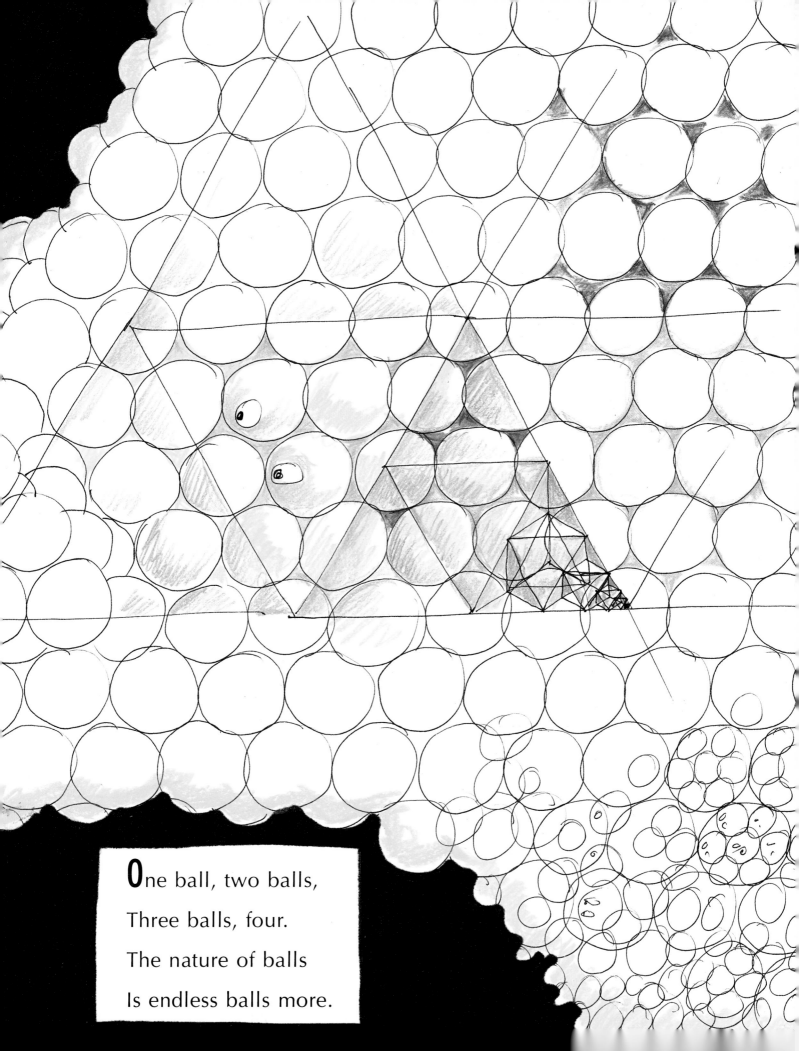

One ball, two balls,

Three balls, four.

The nature of balls

Is endless balls more.

Tetrahedron/octahedron,

Spherical mystery

Of order and patterns

And forming of history.

The WHOLE is all,

And playing with one

Space/time ball

Is infinite fun.

MATERIALS YOU WILL NEED

Lightweight 9-inch–diameter paper plates.

A straightedge for creasing the folds. A ruler works well.

A roll of 3/4-inch masking tape.

12 bobby pins for one sphere.

HINTS FOR FOLDING AND JOINING CIRCLES

◆ Be accurate in placing one point onto another.

◆ Fold and crease well with your straightedge. Strong folded lines
are easy to see and make sharp edges.

◆ Be accurate in folding. It works better and looks better.

◆ Make one fold at a time. Too many layers of paper folded together
will cause inaccurate folds.

◆ When taping point to point, do so in the following way:

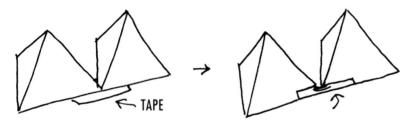

Place two shapes corner to corner, and lay the edges on a piece of tape. Fold the tape over each side and squeeze together in the middle.

◆ When joining edges together, tape the full length.

◆ When taping a hinge joint, put tape on both sides as shown in the
pictures. This gives the greatest range of motion.

2 TETRAHEDRONS

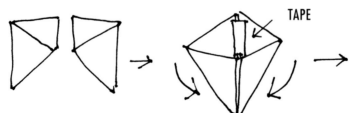

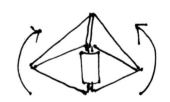

Close face to face, and tape edges together.

Open to opposite sides, and tape reverse sides of edges.

◆ You might use a pencil to emphasize points. It makes them easier
to see at first.

◆ To make the forms more permanent, apply white glue before
taping. Remove tape when glue is dry.